The Usborne
Atlas
of the
World
Picture Book

Sam Baer

Illustrated by Nathalie Ragondet

Designed by Samantha Barrett
with Brenda Cole

Contents

The world

The world is divided into seven large areas of land called continents and five large areas of sea called oceans. The picture maps in this book show amazing animals, places and people from around the world.

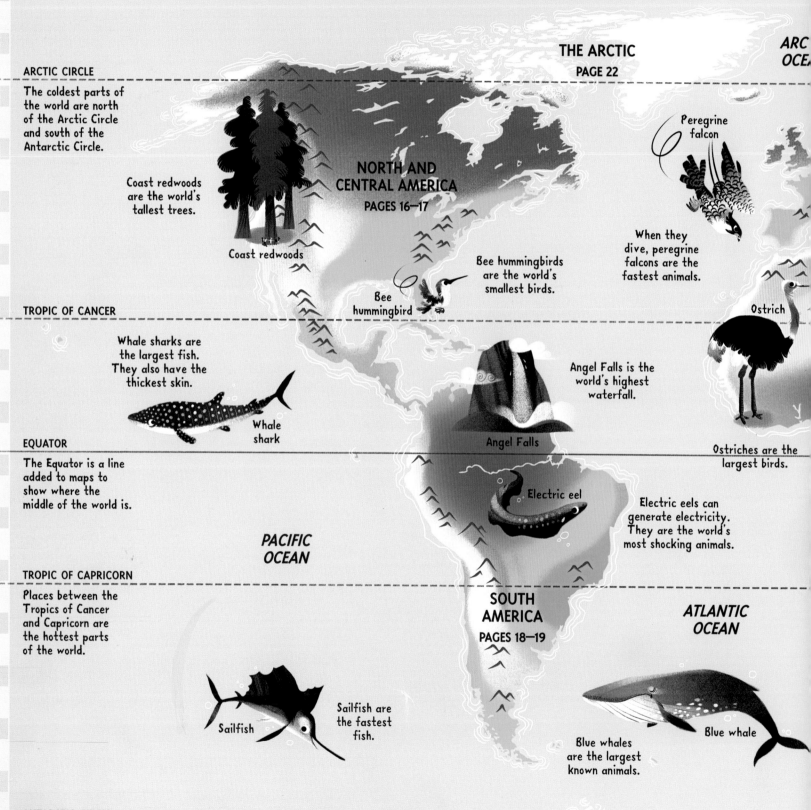

THE ARCTIC
PAGE 22

ARC OCEA

ARCTIC CIRCLE

The coldest parts of the world are north of the Arctic Circle and south of the Antarctic Circle.

Coast redwoods are the world's tallest trees.

Coast redwoods

NORTH AND CENTRAL AMERICA
PAGES 16—17

Peregrine falcon

When they dive, peregrine falcons are the fastest animals.

Bee hummingbirds are the world's smallest birds.

Bee hummingbird

TROPIC OF CANCER

Ostrich

Whale sharks are the largest fish. They also have the thickest skin.

Angel Falls is the world's highest waterfall.

Whale shark

Angel Falls

Ostriches are the largest birds.

EQUATOR

The Equator is a line added to maps to show where the middle of the world is.

Electric eel

Electric eels can generate electricity. They are the world's most shocking animals.

PACIFIC OCEAN

TROPIC OF CAPRICORN

Places between the Tropics of Cancer and Capricorn are the hottest parts of the world.

SOUTH AMERICA
PAGES 18—19

ATLANTIC OCEAN

Sailfish

Sailfish are the fastest fish.

Blue whale

Blue whales are the largest known animals.

ANTARCTIC CIRCLE

SOUTHERN OCEAN

This map shows world record holders, from some of the tallest, smallest and fastest animals to the highest mountain and the longest train line.

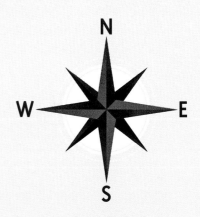

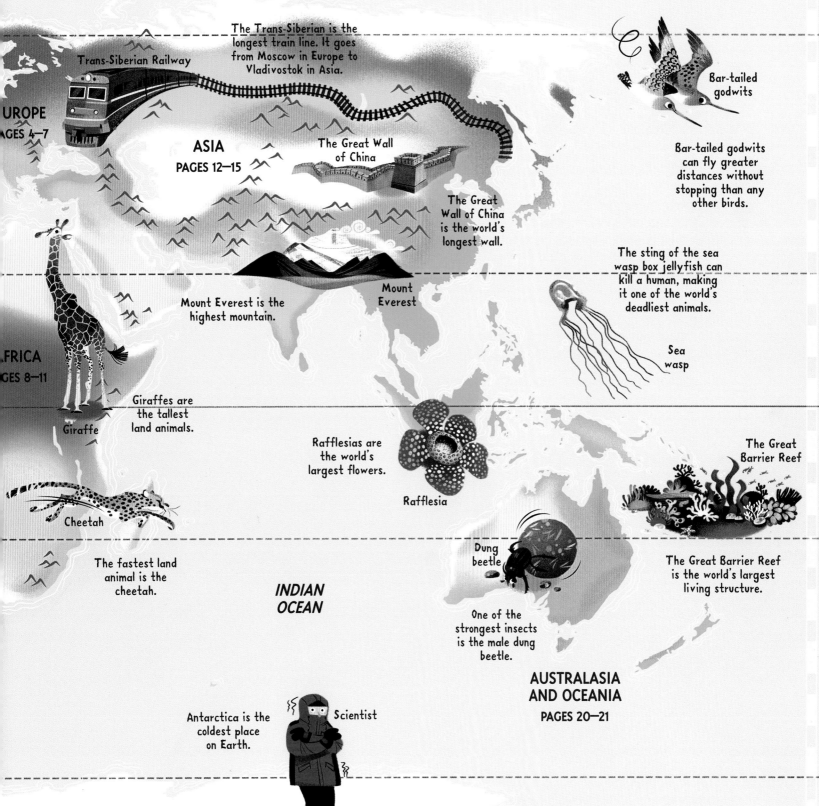

The Trans-Siberian is the longest train line. It goes from Moscow in Europe to Vladivostok in Asia.

Trans-Siberian Railway

EUROPE
PAGES 4—7

ASIA
PAGES 12—15

The Great Wall of China

The Great Wall of China is the world's longest wall.

Mount Everest is the highest mountain.

Mount Everest

Bar-tailed godwits

Bar-tailed godwits can fly greater distances without stopping than any other birds.

The sting of the sea wasp box jellyfish can kill a human, making it one of the world's deadliest animals.

Sea wasp

AFRICA
PAGES 8—11

Giraffes are the tallest land animals.

Giraffe

Rafflesias are the world's largest flowers.

Rafflesia

The Great Barrier Reef

Cheetah

The fastest land animal is the cheetah.

INDIAN OCEAN

Dung beetle

One of the strongest insects is the male dung beetle.

The Great Barrier Reef is the world's largest living structure.

AUSTRALASIA AND OCEANIA
PAGES 20—21

Antarctica is the coldest place on Earth.

Scientist

ANTARCTICA
PAGE 23

Western Europe

Cross-country skiers

ARCTIC CIRCLE

European otter

STOCKHOLM

Midsummer dancers

BALTIC SEA

SWEDEN

Traditional painted wooden horse

ARCTIC OCEAN

NORWEGIAN SEA

Western Europe is shown in pink on this world map.

Fjord horse

NORWAY

Oslo

COPENHAGEN

Stave church

Little Mermaid statue

DENMARK

Mute swan

Cod

SHETLAND ISLANDS

FAROE ISLANDS (DENMARK)

ORKNEY ISLANDS

Bagpipe player

Angel of the North

NORTH SEA

ICELAND

Geyser

Porpoise

UNITED KINGDOM

Dolbadarn Castle

REYKJAVIK

Geysers are jets of hot water and steam that erupt from the ground high into the sky.

European Robin

DUBLIN

Irish dancer

Basking shark

POLAND

White-tailed eagle

BERLIN

Brandenburg Gate

Wild boar with piglet

Puppet show

SLOVAKIA

PRAGUE

CZECH REPUBLIC

VIENNA

Edelweiss flowers

AUSTRIA

HUNGARY

Croatian guard

LJUBLJANA

SLOVENIA

CROATIA

BOSNIA AND HERZEGOVINA

SERBIA

MONTENEGRO

KOSOVO

ALBANIA

Mount Etna is the tallest active volcano in Europe.

SICILY

St. Peter's Cathedral

MALTA

VALLETTA

SAN MARINO

Mount Etna

VADUZ

LIECHTENSTEIN

Leaning Tower of Pisa

BERN

SWITZERLAND

THE ALPS

Alpine marmot

ITALY

ROME

VATICAN CITY

RHINE RIVER

GERMANY

LUXEMBOURG

LUXEMBOURG

European Union headquarters

AMSTERDAM

THE HAGUE

BELGIUM

BRUSSELS

Eiffel Tower

PARIS

FRANCE

Lavender

THE PYRENEES

ANDORRA LA VELLA

ANDORRA

MONACO

CORSICA

SARDINIA

Olives

MEDITERRANEAN SEA

LONDON

Tower Bridge

Camembert cheese

Tour de France cycle rally

BAY OF BISCAY

BALEARIC ISLANDS

The Eden Project

Sagrada Familia Church in Barcelona

Bullfighter with bull

Flamenco dancer

MADRID

SPAIN

Oranges

N
E
S
W

ATLANTIC OCEAN

Belém Tower

LISBON

PORTUGAL

AFRICA

Eastern Europe

Blooms are clouds of microscopic plants that create bright patterns in the sea.

Sea bloom

Wild mushrooms

Eurasian wolves

Sable

Combine harvester

Wheat

URAL MOUNTAINS

Man fishing in ice

ARCTIC OCEAN

Ural owl

Dacha (summer house)

The Russian blue is prized for its silver-blue coat, which feels thick and soft.

Russian blue cat

Gymnast

Fabergé eggs are jewel-covered ornaments. The fanciest eggs were made 100 years ago for the last Russian emperors.

Fabergé eggs

BARENTS SEA

RUSSIA

Moscow

Famous Russian ballets include The Nutcracker, The Firebird, and Swan Lake

Ballet dancers

ARCTIC CIRCLE

VOLGA RIVER

Sparrowhawk

The Winter Palace in St. Petersburg

Santa Claus's post office

FINLAND

Sauna

Elk

HELSINKI

TALLINN

ESTONIA

Seto woman

RIGA

LATVIA

SWEDEN

BALTIC SEA

Walled city of Visby

LITHUANIA

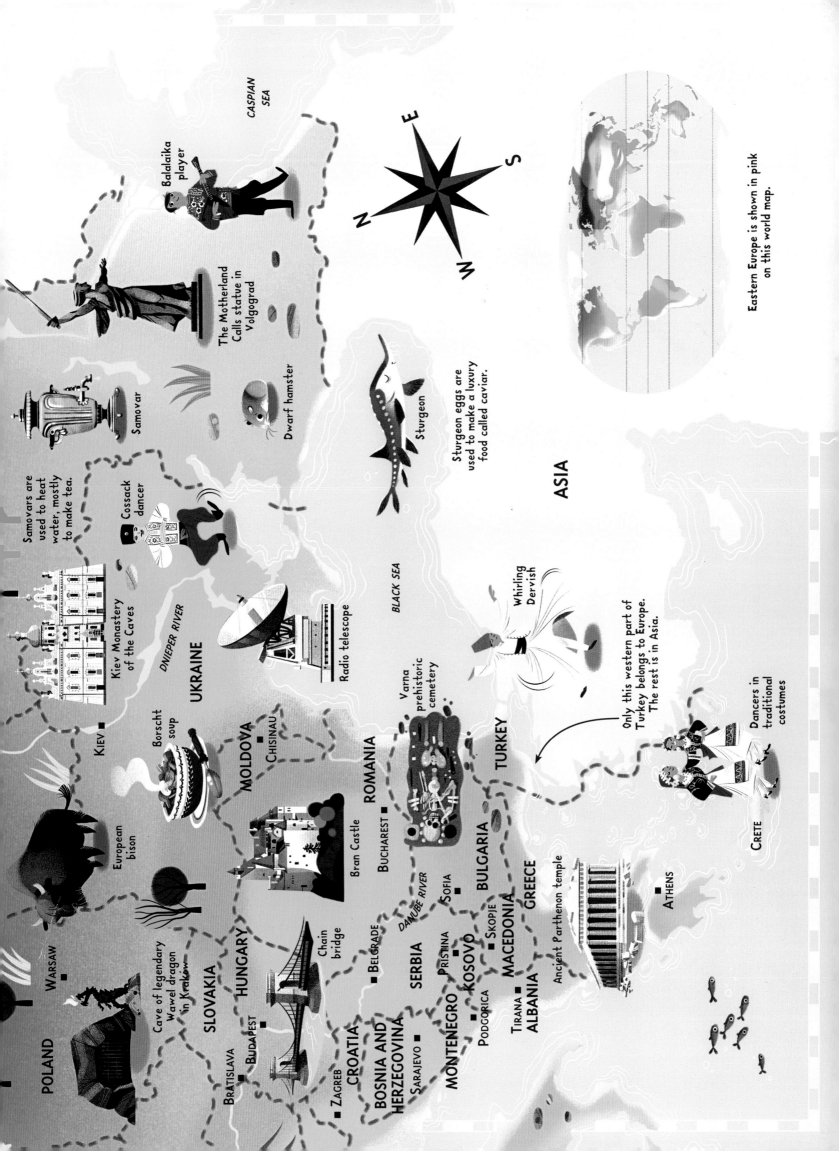

Balalaika player

The Motherland Calls statue in Volgograd

CASPIAN SEA

Samovar

Samovars are used to heat water, mostly to make tea.

Dwarf hamster

Eastern Europe is shown in pink on this world map.

N E S W

Cossack dancer

Kiev Monastery of the Caves

DNIEPER RIVER

UKRAINE

Borscht soup

KIEV

Sturgeon

Sturgeon eggs are used to make a luxury food called caviar.

ASIA

Radio telescope

MOLDOVA
CHISINAU

Varna prehistoric cemetery

BLACK SEA

Whirling Dervish

European bison

Cave of legendary Wawel dragon in Krakow

Bran Castle

ROMANIA

BUCHAREST

Only this western part of Turkey belongs to Europe. The rest is in Asia.

TURKEY

POLAND

WARSAW

SLOVAKIA

BRATISLAVA

HUNGARY

BUDAPEST

Chain bridge

ZAGREB

CROATIA

BOSNIA AND HERZEGOVINA

SARAJEVO

BELGRADE

DANUBE RIVER

SERBIA

PRISTINA

KOSOVO

SOFIA

BULGARIA

SKOPJE

MACEDONIA

GREECE

Ancient Parthenon temple

ATHENS

Dancers in traditional costumes

CRETE

MONTENEGRO

PODGORICA

TIRANA

ALBANIA

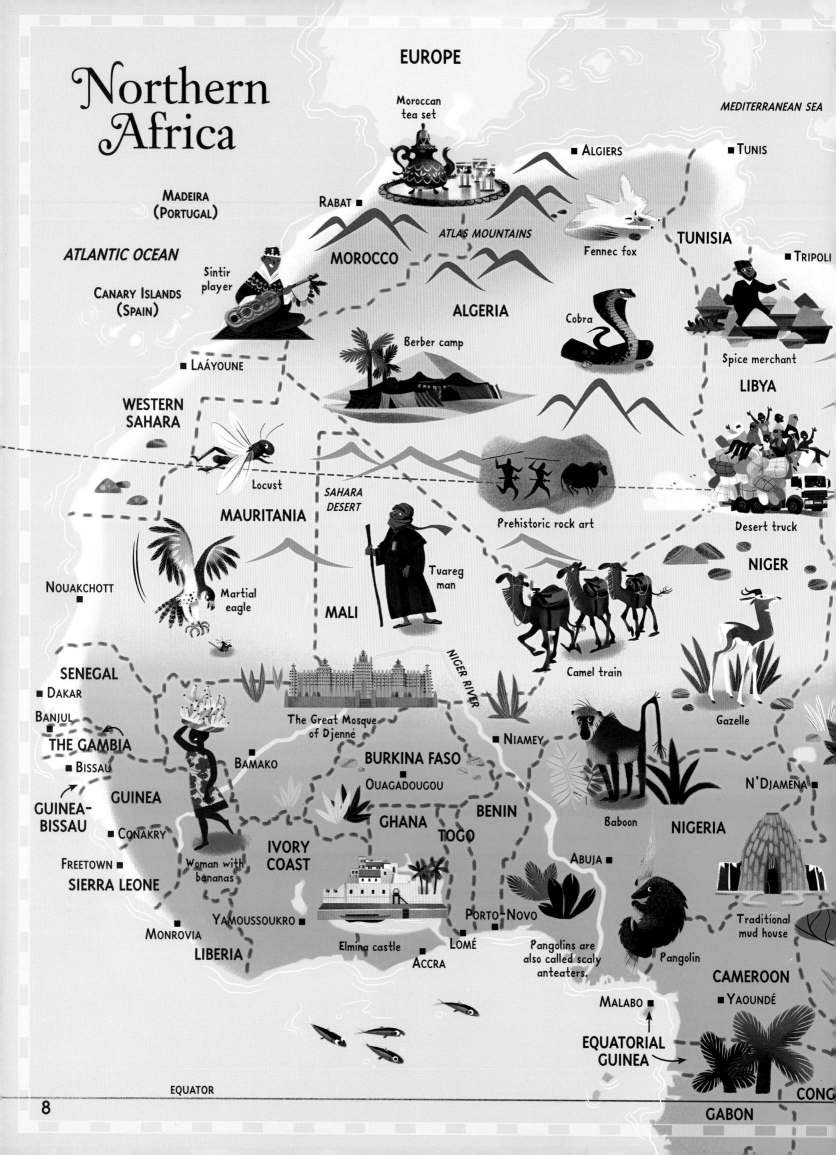

Northern Africa

EUROPE

MEDITERRANEAN SEA

Moroccan tea set

- ALGIERS
- TUNIS

MADEIRA
(PORTUGAL)

- RABAT

ATLAS MOUNTAINS

ATLANTIC OCEAN

Sintir player

MOROCCO

TUNISIA

Fennec fox

- TRIPOLI

CANARY ISLANDS
(SPAIN)

ALGERIA

Cobra

Spice merchant

Berber camp

LIBYA

- LAÁYOUNE

WESTERN
SAHARA

Locust

*SAHARA
DESERT*

Prehistoric rock art

Desert truck

MAURITANIA

Tuareg man

NIGER

- NOUAKCHOTT

Martial eagle

MALI

Camel train

Gazelle

SENEGAL

NIGER RIVER

- DAKAR

The Great Mosque of Djenné

- NIAMEY

Gazelle

BANJUL

BAMAKO

BURKINA FASO

THE GAMBIA

- BISSAU

OUAGADOUGOU

BENIN

Baboon

N'DJAMENA

GUINEA-BISSAU

GUINEA

Woman with bananas

GHANA

TOGO

NIGERIA

- CONAKRY

IVORY COAST

ABUJA

FREETOWN

SIERRA LEONE

YAMOUSSOUKRO

Elmina castle

PORTO-NOVO

LOMÉ

Pangolins are also called scaly anteaters.

Traditional mud house

- MONROVIA

ACCRA

Pangolin

LIBERIA

CAMEROON

MALABO

- YAOUNDÉ

EQUATORIAL
GUINEA

EQUATOR

GABON

CONGO

Seagrass meadow

The pyramids of Giza are around 4,500 years old. Inside each pyramid is a chamber where a king of ancient Egypt was buried.

Northern Africa is shown in pink on this world map.

Oil well

Pyramids of Giza

■ CAIRO

EGYPT

NILE RIVER

RED SEA

ASIA

Jackal

Felucca boat

Scorpion

TROPIC OF CANCER

NUBIAN DESERT

N

CHAD

Gerbil

Crocodile

W   E

SUDAN

ERITREA

S

■ KHARTOUM

■ ASMARA

Date palms

Tamarind fruit is used to make sauces and sweets.

Church of St. George

Tamarind

DJIBOUTI

■ DJIBOUTI

Chameleon

SOMALIA

ADDIS ABABA ■

ETHIOPIA

CENTRAL AFRICAN REPUBLIC

SOUTH SUDAN

Antelope

Karo people

Somali bee-eater

BANGUI

■ JUBA

The Karo people often decorate themselves with body paint.

INDIAN OCEAN

DEMOCRATIC REPUBLIC OF THE CONGO

■ MOGADISHU

African elephant with calf

UGANDA

KENYA

Southern Africa

CAMEROON

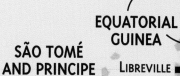

Lovebirds

EQUATORIAL GUINEA

SÃO TOMÉ AND PRINCIPE

LIBREVILLE ■

CONGO

CONGO RIVER

Common octopus

GABON

Mandrill

Chimpanzee sanctuary

An octopus can change its appearance to blend in with its surroundings.

BRAZZAVILLE ■

KINSHASA

ATLANTIC OCEAN

LUANDA ■

Rhinoceros and calf

ANGOLA

Southern Africa is shown in pink on this world map.

Hyena

Yellowfin tuna

Hippopotomus

Hammerhead shark

Prehistoric rock carvings

NAMIBIA

Cargo ship

WINDHOEK ■

Meerkat and pup

N
W   E
S

Portuguese man-of-war

The Portuguese man-of-war has venomous tentacles that can grow up to 50m (165ft) long.

Diamond mining ship

Table Mounta

CAPE TOWN ■

10

An adult male mountain gorilla is called a 'silverback' because of the silver hair on his back and hips.

SUDAN

Coffee beans

ETHIOPIA

SOMALIA

UGANDA

KAMPALA ■

KENYA

Gorilla

Maasai man in traditional dress

NAIROBI ■

EQUATOR

DEMOCRATIC REPUBLIC OF THE CONGO

■ KIGALI

RWANDA

■ BUJUMBURA

BURUNDI

Mount Kilimanjaro

■ DODOMA

■ DAR ES SALAAM

Pitcher plants trap and digest insects in their cup-shaped leaves.

Pitcher plant

SEYCHELLES

Dugong

Safari tour

Lion

TANZANIA

ZAMBIA

Zebra

■ LUSAKA

ZAMBEZI RIVER

Victoria Falls

HARARE ■

ZIMBABWE

Great Zimbabwe

MALAWI

LILONGWE ■

Vulture

MOZAMBIQUE

Wildebeest

Diver

INDIAN OCEAN

■ MORONI

COMOROS

Vanilla orchid

The seeds of the vanilla orchid are used in baking and perfume making.

MADAGASCAR

■ ANTANANARIVO

MAURITIUS

PORT LOUIS ■

RÉUNION (FRANCE)

OTSWANA

These are the ruins of a city that was abandoned 600 years ago.

GABORONE ■

PRETORIA (TSHWANE) ■

■ MAPUTO

Giant clam

Ring-tailed lemur

TROPIC OF CAPRICORN

LOBAMBA ■ ■ MBABANE

SWAZILAND

3LOEMFONTEIN ■

■ MASERU

LESOTHO

Stingray

UTH RICA

Oranges

Cape petrel

11

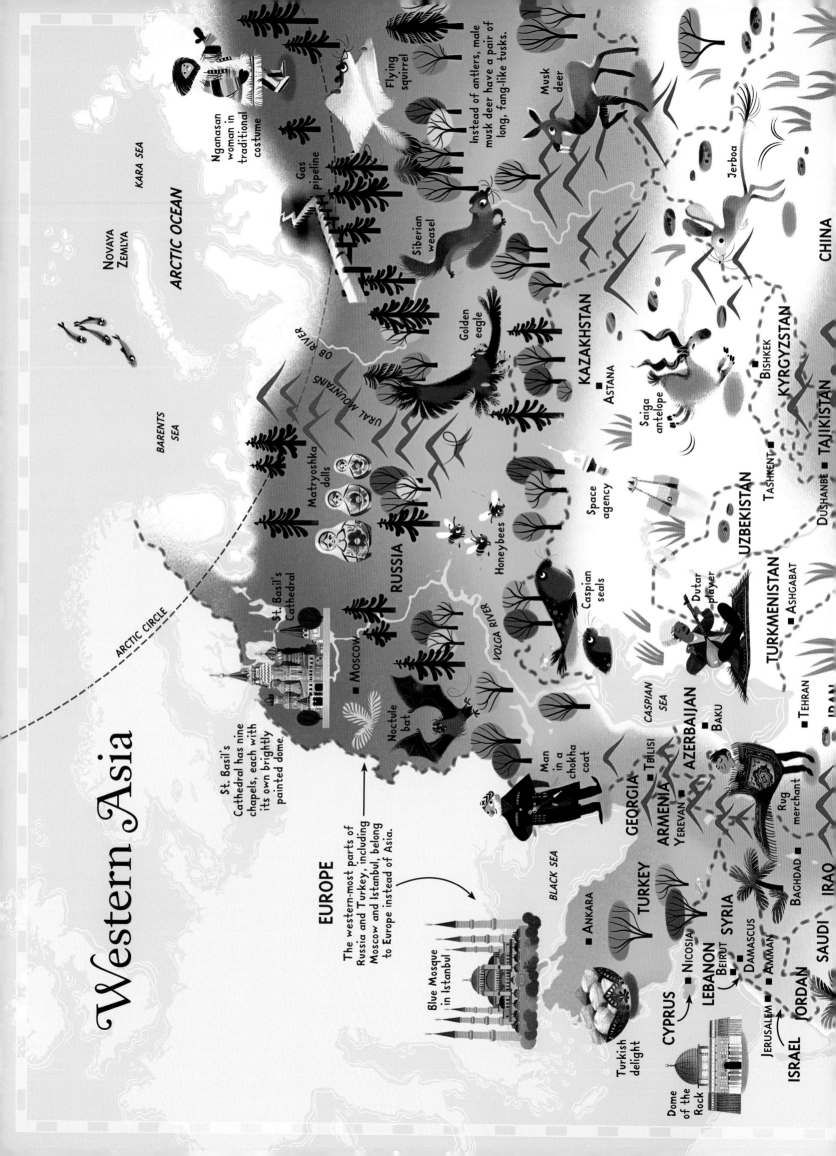

Western Asia

KARA SEA

Nganasan woman in traditional costume

Flying squirrel

Instead of antlers, male musk deer have a pair of long, fang-like tusks.

Musk deer

NOVAYA ZEMLYA

ARCTIC OCEAN

Gas pipeline

Jerboa

Siberian weasel

BARENTS SEA

OB RIVER

Golden eagle

URAL MOUNTAINS

KAZAKHSTAN

■ ASTANA

■ BISHKEK

KYRGYZSTAN

ARCTIC CIRCLE

Matryoshka dolls

Saiga antelope

TASHKENT ■

St. Basil's Cathedral

St. Basil's Cathedral has nine chapels, each with its own brightly painted dome.

RUSSIA

Honeybees

Space agency

UZBEKISTAN

DUSHANBE ■

TAJIKISTAN

Caspian seals

Dutar player

TURKMENISTAN

■ ASHGABAT

■ Moscow

VOLGA RIVER

Noctule bat

CASPIAN SEA

Rug merchant

TEHRAN ■

Man in a chokha coat

AZERBAIJAN

■ BAKU

EUROPE

The western-most parts of Russia and Turkey, including Moscow and Istanbul, belong to Europe instead of Asia.

GEORGIA

ARMENIA

■ TBILISI

IRAN

YEREVAN ■

BLACK SEA

Blue Mosque in Istanbul

TURKEY

■ ANKARA

SYRIA

BAGHDAD ■

Turkish delight

CYPRUS

■ NICOSIA

LEBANON

BEIRUT ■ DAMASCUS ■

■ AMMAN

SAUDI

IRAQ

Dome of the Rock

ISRAEL

JERUSALEM ■

JORDAN

CHINA

Tibetan monk

BURMA

BHUTAN

THE HIMALAYAS

Mount Everest

Red panda

NEPAL

BANGLADESH

GANGES RIVER

Bengal tiger

BAY OF BENGAL

The lotus is the national flower of India. It's used in traditional medicine and cooking.

N
E
W
S

Tea

Taj Mahal

■ New Delhi

Lotus flower

Sri Jayewardenepura Kotte
■ SRI LANKA

Colombo ■

ISLAMABAD ■

PAKISTAN

Girl in a sari

INDUS RIVER

Rickshaw

TAXI

INDIA

Sawfish

Afghan hound

MALDIVES

MALÉ ■

Ruins of ancient Persepolis

Muscat ■

Sea snakes have flat, paddle-shaped tails that help them to swim.

ARABIAN SEA

INDIAN OCEAN

Abu Dhabi ■

UNITED ARAB EMIRATES

QATAR
■ DOHA

Arabian Gulf sea snake

Tiger shark

BAHRAIN

OMAN

Oil drilling rig

RIYADH ■

Arabian horse

Socotra

Arabian dhow boats

The Kaaba in Mecca

SANA'A ■

YEMEN

RED SEA

AFRICA

EQUATOR

Western Asia is shown in pink on this world map

TROPIC OF CANCER

Eastern Asia

PACIFIC OCEAN

Humpback whale

Puffer fish

Crane

Bullet train

Cherry blossom tree

BERING SEA

Brown bear

SEA OF OKHOTSK

Ringed seal

JAPAN
■ Tokyo

Sumo wrestler

Russian Orthodox cathedral

The Forbidden City was the private home of emperors for almost 500 years.

NORTH KOREA

■ PYONGYANG

SEOUL ■

SOUTH

ARCTIC CIRCLE

WRANGEL ISLAND

Snow geese

Siberian tigers

Tai chi expert

Forbidden City

BEIJING ■

EAST SIBERIAN SEA

NEW SIBERIAN ISLANDS

LENA RIVER

RUSSIA

Buryat girl in traditional costume

LAKE BAIKAL

NOVAYA ZEMLYA

SEVERNAYA ZEMLYA

LAPTEV SEA

KARA SEA

Putorana Plateau

Siberian chipmunk

Sayano–Shushenskaya dam

MONGOLIA

■ ULAN BATOR

Ger (tent)

Bactrian camel

GOBI DESERT

YENISEY RIVER

Man with a fur hat

The Sayano–Shushenskaya dam is the largest power plant in Russia.

KAZAKHSTAN

Rice bowl with chopsticks

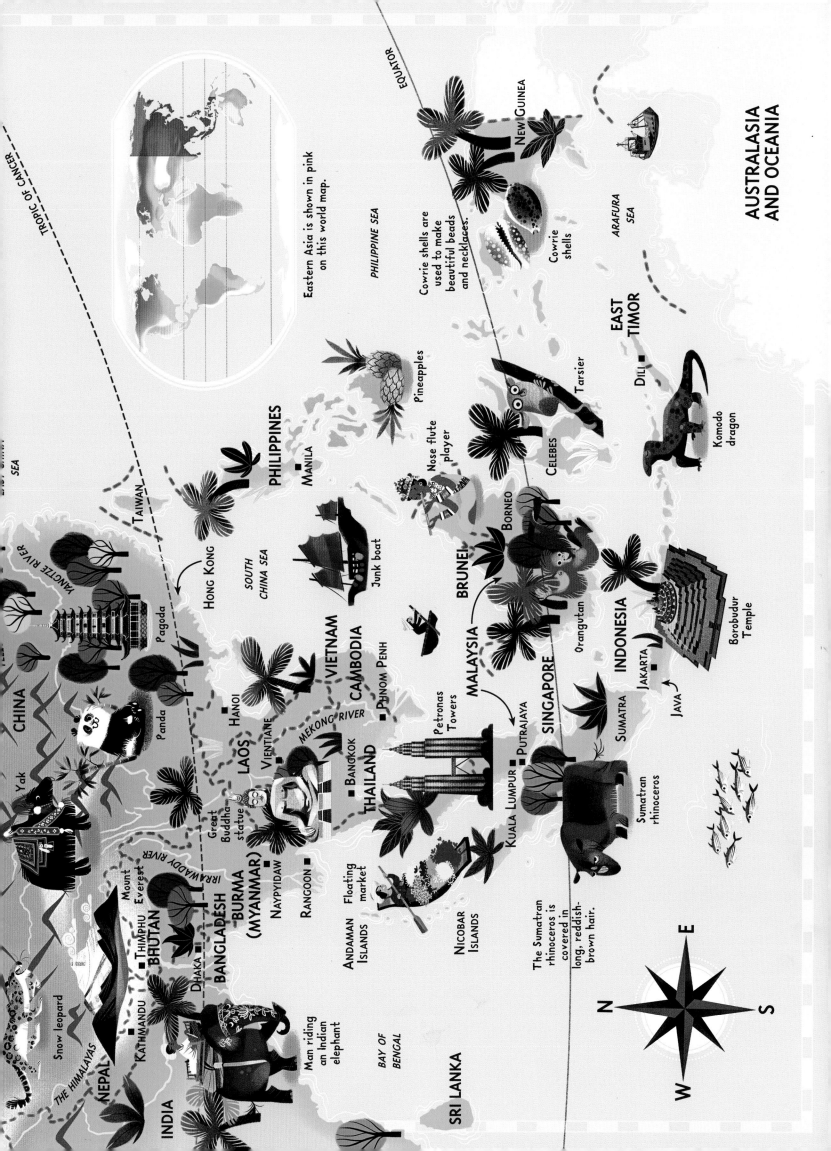

AUSTRALASIA AND OCEANIA

TROPIC OF CANCER

Eastern Asia is shown in pink on this world map.

EQUATOR

NEW GUINEA

PHILIPPINE SEA

Cowrie shells are used to make beautiful beads and necklaces.

Cowrie shells

ARAFURA SEA

EAST TIMOR

DILI

Komodo dragon

Pineapples

Tarsier

CELEBES

Nose flute player

MANILA

PHILIPPINES

TAIWAN

BORNEO

BRUNEI

Orangutan

INDONESIA

Borobudur Temple

JAKARTA

JAVA

Hong Kong

Pagoda

SOUTH CHINA SEA

Junk boat

MALAYSIA

PUTRAJAYA

KUALA LUMPUR

SINGAPORE

Petronas Towers

SUMATRA

Sumatran rhinoceros

The Sumatran rhinoceros is covered in long, reddish-brown hair.

CHINA

YANGTZE RIVER

Panda

Yak

VIETNAM

CAMBODIA

PHNOM PENH

HANOI

LAOS

VIENTIANE

MEKONG RIVER

THAILAND

BANGKOK

Great Buddha statue

Floating market

NICOBAR ISLANDS

Snow leopard

THE HIMALAYAS

Mount Everest

NEPAL

KATHMANDU

THIMPHU

BHUTAN

DHAKA

BANGLADESH

BURMA (MYANMAR)

NAYPYIDAW

RANGOON

IRRAWADDY RIVER

ANDAMAN ISLANDS

BAY OF BENGAL

Man riding an Indian elephant

INDIA

SRI LANKA

N
W   E
S

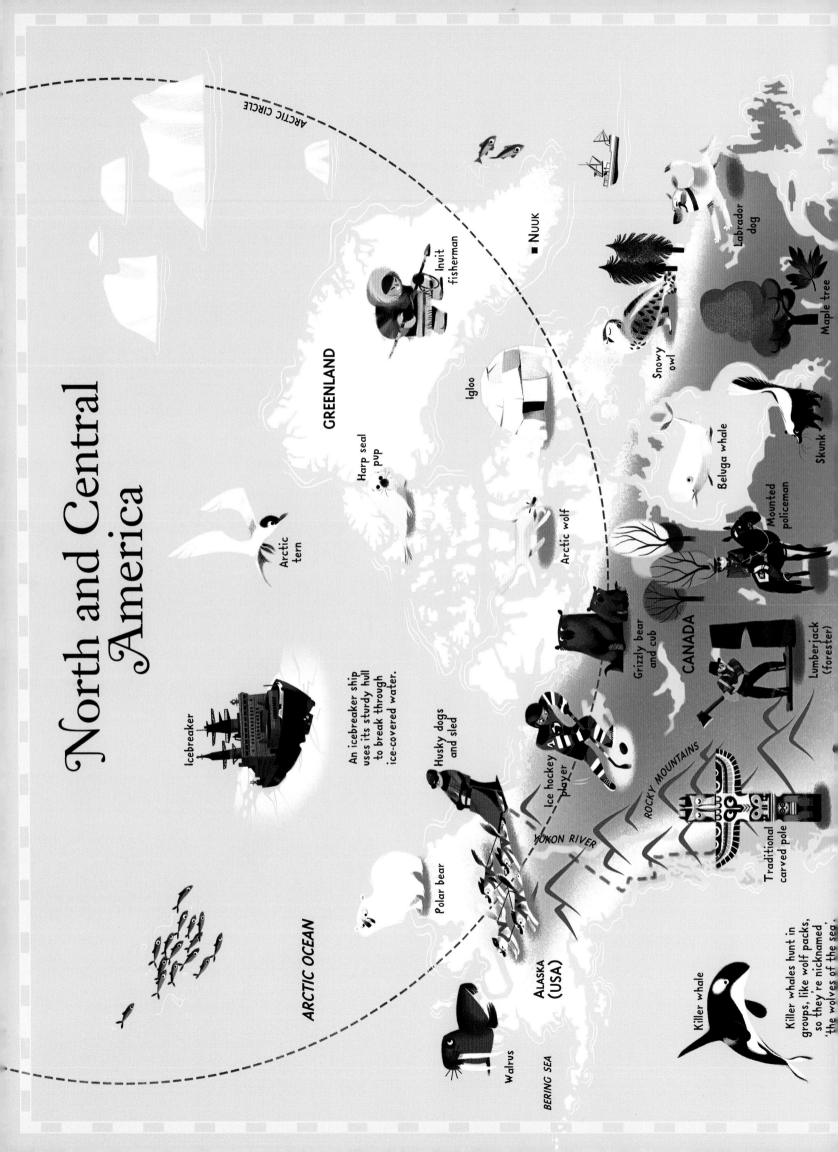

North and Central America

ARCTIC CIRCLE

Nuuk

GREENLAND

Inuit fisherman

Igloo

Harp seal pup

Arctic tern

Snowy owl

Labrador dog

Maple tree

Beluga whale

Skunk

Arctic wolf

Mounted policeman

Icebreaker

An icebreaker ship uses its sturdy hull to break through ice-covered water.

Husky dogs and sled

Grizzly bear and cub

CANADA

Lumberjack (forester)

ARCTIC OCEAN

Polar bear

Ice hockey player

ROCKY MOUNTAINS

YUKON RIVER

Traditional carved pole

Walrus

Alaska (USA)

BERING SEA

Killer whale

Killer whales hunt in groups, like wolf packs, so they're nicknamed 'the wolves of the sea'.

Golden Gate Bridge in San Francisco

The Grand Canyon

Bald eagle

American bison

RIVER

Jumbo jet

A jumbo jet is so big it can carry over 400 passengers.

Hopi dancer

Mexican musician

Donkey

RIO GRANDE RIVER

Monarch butterfly

TROPIC OF CANCER

PACIFIC OCEAN

Common dolphins

UNITED STATES OF AMERICA

GREAT LAKES

American football player

WASHINGTON DC

The White House

MISSISSIPPI RIVER

Alligator

The Statue of Liberty in New York

The Statue of Liberty was given to the USA by France in 1886 as a symbol of friendship.

ATLANTIC OCEAN

Space Center

THE BAHAMAS

HAVANA ■ CUBA

Mexico City ■ MEXICO

Mayan temple

BELIZE ■ Belmopan

GUATEMALA
Guatemala City ■

HONDURAS
■ Tegucigalpa

San Salvador ■ NICARAGUA
EL SALVADOR ■ Managua

COSTA RICA
San José ■

Howler monkey

DOMINICAN REPUBLIC

PUERTO RICO (USA)

HAITI

JAMAICA

Reggae musician

CARIBBEAN SEA

PANAMA
● Panama City

SOUTH AMERICA

North and Central America are shown in pink on this world map.

N
W E
S

South America

NORTH AND CENTRAL AMERICA

Maracas have been used in Colombian music for over 1,500 years.

CARIBBEAN SEA

Hawksbill turtle

Maracas

COLOMBIA

■ BOGOTÁ

Peccaries

■ QUITO

ECUADOR

Boy in a poncho

Llama

■ LIMA

Machu Picchu is a mountain city built 600 years ago by people known as Incas.

Machu Picchu

Great white shark

Great white sharks can sense blood in the water up to 5km (3 miles) away.

EQUATOR

Rocket base

Oil platform

■ CARACAS

VENEZUELA

Angel Falls

GEORGETOWN ■

GUYANA

PARAMARIBO ■

SURINAME

FRENCH GUIANA

CAYENNE ■

Spider monkey

Sloth

AMAZON RIVER

Poison dart frog

Blue morpho butterfly

BOLIVIA

Spectacled bear

Cocoa beans are used to make chocolate. They come from the seed pods of the cacao tree.

Capoeira experts

Scarlet macaws

Cocoa pods

River dolphin

Anaconda

BRAZIL

AMAZON RAINFOREST

Jaguar

Gemstone mining

Orchid

BRASILIA ■

Brasilia Cathedral

Statue of Christ the Redeemer in Rio de Janeiro

ATLANTIC OCEAN

Rio carnival is an annual street festival where people dress up in bright costumes and dance.

Humpback anglerfish

South America is shown in pink on this world map.

Carnival dancer

Giant anteater

Queen triggerfish

Caiman

PARAGUAY

URUGUAY

■ MONTEVIDEO

Albatrosses have larger wingspans than any other bird.

ASUNCIÓN

ARGENTINA

BUENOS AIRES

Albatrosses

FALKLAND ISLANDS (UK)

THE ANDES MOUNTAINS

Tango dancers

Gaucho (cowboy)

Magellanic penguin

ATACAMA DESERT

CHILE

Armadillo

CAPE HORN

SANTIAGO ■

Monkey puzzle tree

Fur seal

Rockhopper penguins

Flamingos

TROPIC OF CAPRICORN

PACIFIC OCEAN

Opah

N E S W

Australasia and Oceania

NORTHERN MARIANA ISLANDS (USA)

GUAM (USA)

KOROR ■

The Mariana Trench

The Mariana Trench is found far underwater. It is the deepest place in the world.

PALIKIR ■

Lionfish

PALAU

FEDERATED STATES OF MICRONESIA

Sacred house

Clown fish

ASIA

NEW GUINEA

PAPUA NEW GUINEA

■ PORT MORESBY

HONIARA ■

INDIAN OCEAN

ARAFURA SEA

Funnel-web spider

Great Barrier Reef

CORAL SEA

Bottlenose dolphin

Kangaroo and joey (baby)

Frilled lizard

The didgeridoo is a wind instrument that has been used by native Australians for around 1,500 years.

Didgeridoo player

GREAT SANDY DESERT

AUSTRALIA

Platypus

Flying doctor

Uluru (Ayers Rock)

Koala

A koala can sleep for up to 18 hours a day.

Sydney Opera House

GREAT VICTORIA DESERT

DARLING RIVER

Emu

Black swan and cygnet

Mining for opals (precious stones)

CANBERRA ■

MURRAY RIVER

N E W S

Surfer

TASMANIA (AUSTRALIA)

Tasmanian devil

TASMAN SEA

Cruise ship

Hula dancer

HAWAIIAN
ISLANDS
(USA)

Seahorse

MARSHALL
ISLANDS

PACIFIC OCEAN

Manta rays use
wing-like fins to glide
through the water and
leap above the surface.

■ MAJURO

Ribbon eel

■ BAIRIKI

Flying fish

LINE ISLANDS

Manta ray

■ YAREN

Outrigger
canoe

EQUATOR

NAURU

KIRIBATI

■ FUNAFUTI

Seaplane

Swordfish

SOLOMON
ISLANDS

TUVALU

TOKELAU
(NZ)

VANUATU

SAMOA

WALLIS AND FUTUNA
(FRANCE)

AMERICAN
SAMOA
(USA)

Leatherback
turtle

MARQUESAS
ISLANDS

■ PORT VILA

■ SUVA

■ APIA

FIJI

Hunga Tonga
underwater
volcano

The leatherback is
the largest species
of turtle.

NEW CALEDONIA
(FRANCE)

Rugby
player

NUKU'ALOFA

NIUE
(NZ)

FRENCH POLYNESIA
(FRANCE)

SOCIETY
ISLANDS

TONGA

COOK ISLANDS
(NZ)

Sperm
whale

Kiwi bird

Australasian
gannet

Maori
dancer

TROPIC OF CAPRICORN

NEW ZEALAND

PITCAIRN
ISLANDS
(UK)

■ WELLINGTON

Sheep with
lambs

Australasia and Oceania are shown
in pink on this world map.

21

The Arctic

BERING SEA

SEA OF OKHOTSK

GULF OF ALASKA

Kamchatka volcanoes

Chukchi tent

ALASKA (USA)

NORTH AND CENTRAL AMERICA

Lynx

ARCTIC CIRCLE

ASIA

WRANGEL ISLAND

CHUKCHI SEA

Ptarmigan

Wolverine

BEAUFORT SEA

ARCTIC OCEAN

CANADA

Submarine laboratory

NEW SIBERIAN ISLANDS

Ermine

Musk ox

Arctic hare

There is no land at the North Pole, only a thick layer of ice that covers most of the Arctic Ocean.

LAPTEV SEA

Explorer

RUSSIA

SEVERNAYA ZEMLYA

Arctic poppies

● NORTH POLE

Reindeer with sled

ELLESMERE ISLAND

A male narwhal's tusk is longer than an adult human is tall.

KARA SEA

Northern lights

FRANZ JOSEF LAND

BAFFIN ISLAND

Narwhal

Lemming

Fishing village

Carved figurine

GREENLAND

SVALBARD

NOVAYA ZEMLYA

BARENTS SEA

NUUK ■

Research boat

Woman in traditional costume

Sami people

SWEDEN

Puffin

NORWAY FINLAND

EUROPE

Ice hotel

ICELAND

ATLANTIC OCEAN

Antarctica

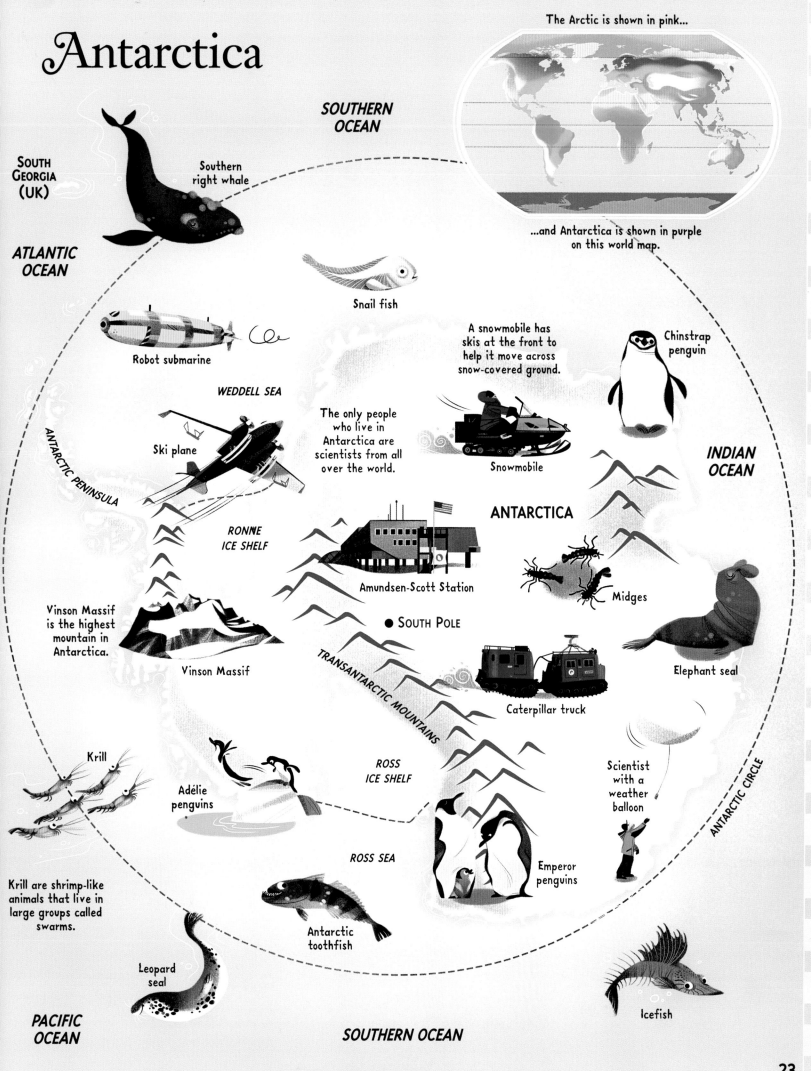

The Arctic is shown in pink...

...and Antarctica is shown in purple on this world map.

SOUTHERN OCEAN

SOUTH GEORGIA (UK)

ATLANTIC OCEAN

Southern right whale

Snail fish

Robot submarine

A snowmobile has skis at the front to help it move across snow-covered ground.

WEDDELL SEA

The only people who live in Antarctica are scientists from all over the world.

Ski plane

Snowmobile

ANTARCTIC PENINSULA

Chinstrap penguin

INDIAN OCEAN

RONNE ICE SHELF

ANTARCTICA

Amundsen-Scott Station

Midges

Vinson Massif is the highest mountain in Antarctica.

SOUTH POLE

Vinson Massif

Elephant seal

TRANSANTARCTIC MOUNTAINS

Caterpillar truck

Krill

ROSS ICE SHELF

Scientist with a weather balloon

Adélie penguins

ANTARCTIC CIRCLE

Krill are shrimp-like animals that live in large groups called swarms.

ROSS SEA

Emperor penguins

Leopard seal

Antarctic toothfish

Icefish

PACIFIC OCEAN

SOUTHERN OCEAN

Flags of the world

There are 195 recognized independent states in the world, and each one has its own flag that is used to represent it overseas. These pages show each of these flags, arranged by continent. Russia and Turkey are regarded as being part of both Europe and Asia.

Europe PAGES 4–7

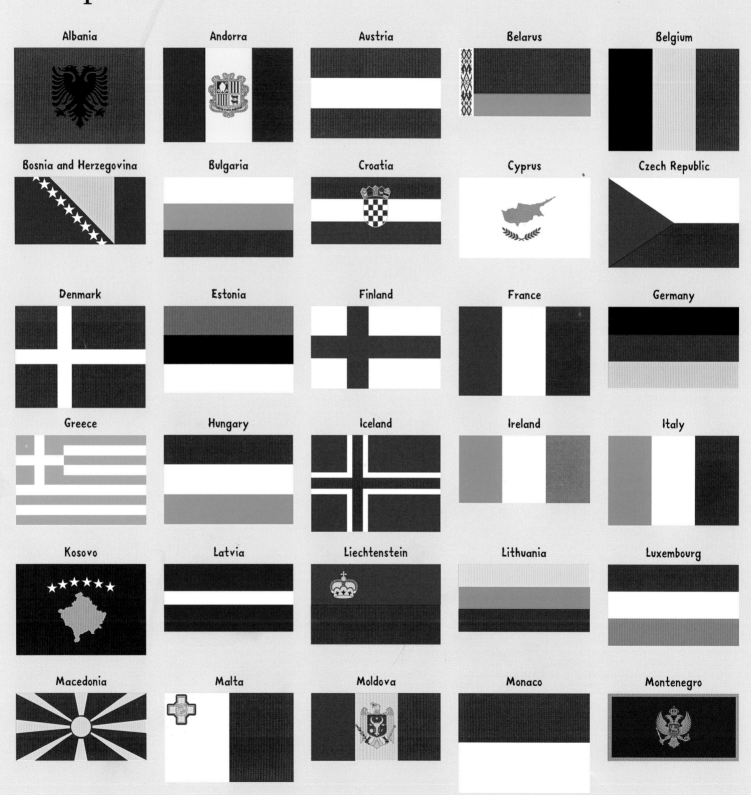

Albania	Andorra	Austria	Belarus	Belgium
Bosnia and Herzegovina	Bulgaria	Croatia	Cyprus	Czech Republic
Denmark	Estonia	Finland	France	Germany
Greece	Hungary	Iceland	Ireland	Italy
Kosovo	Latvia	Liechtenstein	Lithuania	Luxembourg
Macedonia	Malta	Moldova	Monaco	Montenegro

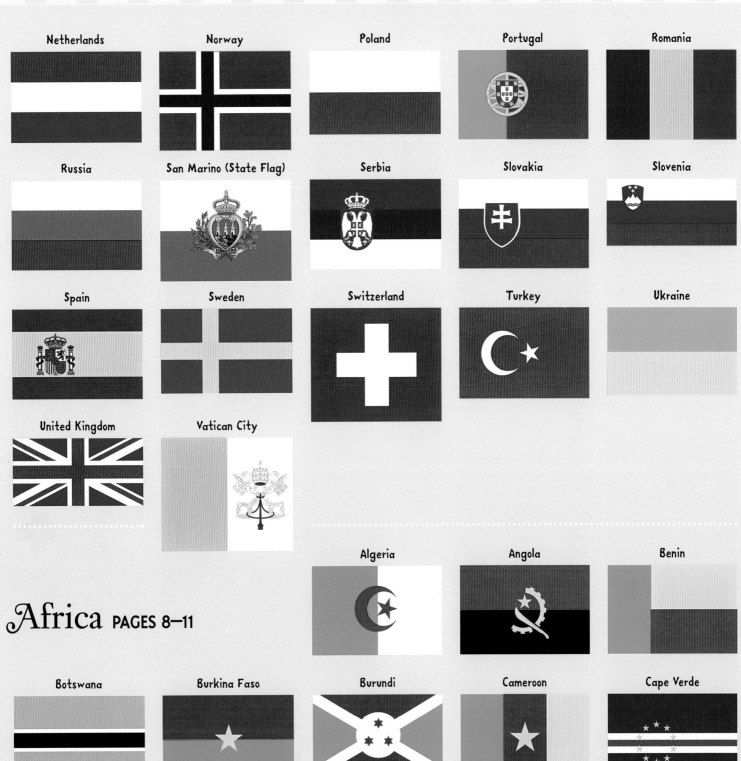

Netherlands
Norway
Poland
Portugal
Romania

Russia
San Marino (State Flag)
Serbia
Slovakia
Slovenia

Spain
Sweden
Switzerland
Turkey
Ukraine

United Kingdom
Vatican City

Africa PAGES 8–11

Algeria
Angola
Benin

Botswana
Burkina Faso
Burundi
Cameroon
Cape Verde

Central African Republic
Chad
Comoros
Congo-Brazzaville
Congo, Democratic Republic of

Djibouti
Egypt
Equitorial Guinea
Eritrea
Ethiopia

Africa
PAGES 8–11
(CONTINUED)

Gabon

Gambia, The

Ghana

Guinea

Guinea-Bissau

Ivory Coast (Cote d'Ivoire)

Kenya

Lesotho

Liberia

Libya

Madagascar

Malawi

Mali

Mauritania

Mauritius

Morocco

Mozambique

Namibia

Niger

Nigeria

Rwanda

Sao Tome and Principe

Senegal

Seychelles

Sierra Leone

Somalia

South Africa

South Sudan

Sudan

Swaziland

Tanzania

Togo

Tunisia

Uganda

Zambia

Zimbabwe

Asia
PAGES 12–15

Afghanistan

Armenia
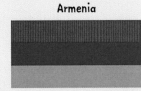

Azerbaijan

Bahrain

Bangladesh

Bhutan

Brunei

Burma (Myanmar)

Cambodia

China

East Timor (Timor-Leste)

Georgia
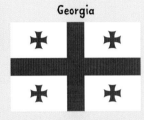

India
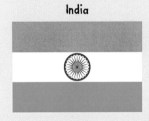

Indonesia

Iran

Iraq

Israel

Japan

Jordan

Kazakhstan

Kuwait
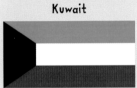

Kyrgyzstan

Laos
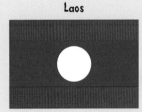

Lebanon

Malaysia

Maldives

Mongolia

Nepal

North Korea

Oman

Pakistan

Philippines

Qatar

Russia

Saudi Arabia

Singapore

South Korea

Sri Lanka

Asia

PAGES 12–15
(CONTINUED)

Syria

Tajikistan

Thailand

Turkey

Turkmenistan

United Arab Emirates

Uzbekistan

Vietnam

Yemen

North and Central America
PAGES 16–17

Antigua and Barbuda

Bahamas, The

Barbados

Belize

Canada

Costa Rica

Cuba

Dominica

Dominican Republic

El Salvador

Grenada

Guatemala

Haiti

Honduras

Jamaica

Mexico

Nicaragua

Panama

Saint Kitts and Nevis
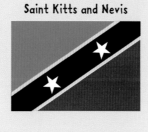

Saint Lucia

Saint Vincent and the Grenadines

Trinidad and Tobago

United States of America

South America
PAGES 18–19

Argentina

Bolivia

Brazil

Chile

Colombia

Ecuador
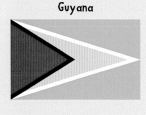

Guyana

Paraguay

Peru

Suriname

Uruguay

Venezuela

Australasia and Oceania
PAGES 20–21

Australia

Fiji

Kiribati

Marshall Islands

Micronesia, Federated States of

Nauru
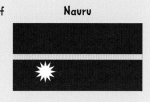

New Zealand

Palau

Papua New Guinea

Samoa

Solomon Islands

Tonga

Tuvalu
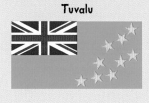

Vanuatu

The Arctic and Antarctica
PAGES 22–23

Different parts of the Arctic belong to different countries: Canada, Norway, Russia, Denmark and the United States. The rest is unowned and has no flag. Antarctica is not officially owned by any country and has no flag of its own.

World quiz

Here are some of the fascinating things that can be seen around the world.
Which maps can you find them on? The answers are at the bottom of the page.

Poison dart frog

White-tailed eagle

Chimpanzee sanctuary

Pangolin

European bison

Eiffel Tower

Forbidden City

Taj Mahal

Statue of Liberty

St. Basil's Cathedral

Bactrian camel

Meerkat and pup

Pyramids of Giza

Frilled lizard

The Grand Canyon

Diver

Puffer fish

Outrigger canoe

Southern right whale

Hawksbill turtle

Ringed seal

Inuit fisherman

Arctic poppies

Emperor penguins

Cross-country skiers

Answers: Poison dart frog, South America; White-tailed eagle, Western Europe; Chimpanzee sanctuary, Southern Africa; Pangolin, Northern Africa;
European bison, Eastern Europe; Eiffel Tower, Western Europe; Forbidden City, Eastern Asia; Taj Mahal, Western Asia; Statue of Liberty, North and
Central America; St. Basil's Cathedral, Eastern Europe; Bactrian camel, Eastern Asia; Meerkat and pup, Southern Africa; Pyramids of Giza, Northern
Africa; Frilled lizard, Australasia and Oceania; The Grand Canyon, North and Central America; Diver, Southern Africa; Puffer fish, Eastern Asia;
Outrigger canoe, Australasia and Oceania; Southern right whale, Antarctica; Hawksbill turtle, South America; Ringed seal, Eastern Asia; Inuit fisherman,
North and Central America; Arctic poppies, The Arctic; Emperor penguins, Antarctica; Cross-country skiers, Western Europe.

Index

Internet Links

For links to websites where you can find out more about places, people and animals around the world, go to Usborne Quicklinks at www.usborne.com/quicklinks and type the keywords 'Atlas of the World picture book'.

Digital manipulation by Nick Wakeford
Managing Editor: Ruth Brocklehurst   Managing Designer: Stephen Moncrieff

This edition first published in 2015 by Usborne Publishing Ltd., Usborne House, 83-85 Saffron Hill, London, EC1N 8RT, England. www.usborne.com Copyright © 2015, 2013 Usborne Publishing Ltd.